# WHAT'S YOUR ANGLE, PYTHAGORAS?

A Math Adventure

by Julie Ellis

illustrated by Phyllis Hornung

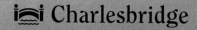 Charlesbridge

To Tim for patiently helping me with the math concepts, and to Olive for hours of babysitting. — J.E.

For Chris — P.H.

Text copyright © 2004 by Julie Ellis
Illustrations copyright © 2004 by Phyllis Hornung
Published by Charlesbridge Publishing, 85 Main Street, Watertown, MA 02472
(617) 926-0329 • www.charlesbridge.com

Printed in Korea
(sc) 10 9 8 7 6 5 4 3 2 1
(hc) 10 9 8 7 6 5 4 3 2 1

**Library of Congress Cataloging-in-Publication Data**
Ellis, Julie, 1961-
What's your angle, Pythagoras? : a math adventure / by Julie Ellis ;
illustrated by Phyllis Hornung.
    p. cm.
    Summary: In ancient Greece, young Pythagoras discovers a special number
pattern (the Pythagorean theorem) and uses it to solve problems
involving right triangles.
    ISBN 1-57091-150-9 (Softcover)
    ISBN 1-57091-197-5 (Hardcover)
    1. Pythagorean theorem—Juvenile literature.
[1. Pythagorean theorem.  2. Geometry.]
I. Hornung, Phyllis, ill. II. Title.
QA460.P8 E38 2002
516.22—dc21
2002002380

Long ago in ancient Greece, there lived a curious boy named Pythagoras.

Pythagoras just couldn't help poking his nose into places. Sometimes, his curiosity got him in trouble, but sometimes it paid off.

3

One day, Pythagoras sat in the shade of an old olive tree. He could see the harbor and the sparkling blue sea around the island where he lived.

Nearby, two workmen were building a temple. They began to argue. "This ladder is too short to reach the roof," Pepros grumbled.

"That's not possible," said Saltos. "The wall is 12 feet tall, so I made the ladder 12 feet long."

Pepros roared, "The ladder only reaches the roof when it is flat against the wall, and then no one can climb it! This is as bad as the columns on the porch!"

Pythagoras poked his head out from behind the tree. "What's wrong with the columns?" he asked.

4

Pepros frowned.
"It's that pesky
Pythagoras again.

"Stop bothering us!
At this rate, we'll never
finish the temple!"

5

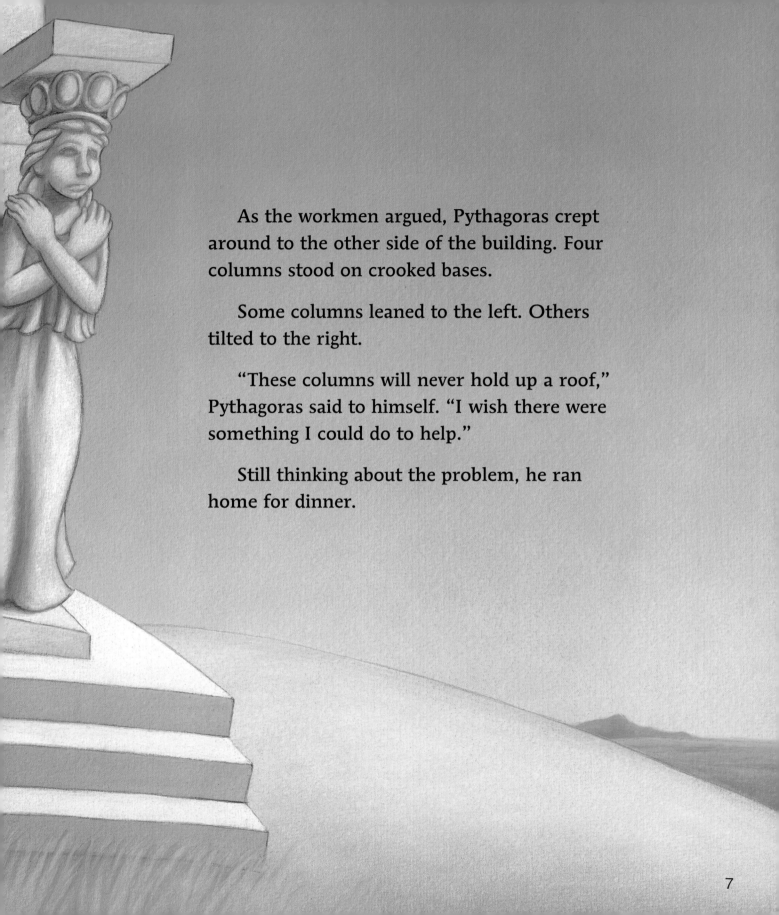

As the workmen argued, Pythagoras crept around to the other side of the building. Four columns stood on crooked bases.

Some columns leaned to the left. Others tilted to the right.

"These columns will never hold up a roof," Pythagoras said to himself. "I wish there were something I could do to help."

Still thinking about the problem, he ran home for dinner.

When he got home, his father was talking about his ship.

"I sailed to Crete with a shipload of tiles, but Leapus and Boundus got there before me. With their fast new ship they will take away all my customers."

Through a mouthful of bread and olives, Pythagoras asked, "Father, you always sail to Rhodes first and then to Crete. Why don't you just sail straight from here to Crete? It would be a lot faster."

"It's too dangerous," his father replied. "It would not be safe to sail straight from here to Crete, unless I knew the exact distance. Out at sea, I could miss Crete and end up anywhere!

"I'm leaving for Egypt tomorrow. I want you to come with me, son. One day you will command my merchant ships, and you have much to learn."

At dawn the next morning,
Pythagoras and his father set sail.
As they sailed along the coast,
Pythagoras said,
"I can't wait to
see Alexandria!
I hear they have great
buildings there. I might
want to be a builder
someday."

"But, son, you are going to be a merchant," his father said. "The life of a merchant is exciting. You get to sail to faraway places." He put an arm around Pythagoras's shoulders, "You just have to look at it from the right angle."

Soon they were sailing into the port of Alexandria, the capital city of Egypt. Pythagoras marveled at the great lighthouse that stood proudly against the sky. "Saltos and Pepros should see this!" he exclaimed.

At the dock, a man greeted them. "I am the builder Neferheperhersekeper, but people call me Nef. I'm here for the tiles."

Pythagoras was excited to meet a real builder. "Have you built anything around here?" he asked.

Nef nodded. "As a matter of fact, I helped to build the lighthouse."

"How did you get the base so straight?" Pythagoras asked, thinking of the crooked columns back at home. "You must be a master builder."

Nef smiled and stuck out his chest. "The secret is this special rope that's been used by my family for ages."

"You use a knotted rope to cut stone?" Pythagoras asked.

Nef laughed. "My dear boy, this rope does not cut stone! I use the rope to make a special triangle. I call it the 'right triangle' because it helps me make a nice, square corner that's exactly the right angle for cutting stone."

Nef let Pythagoras hold the rope. Pythagoras made some triangles, but none had the right angle. "How long do you make each side?" he asked.

"Oh, I've shown you too much already," chuckled Nef, as he took back his rope. "Why don't you run along now?"

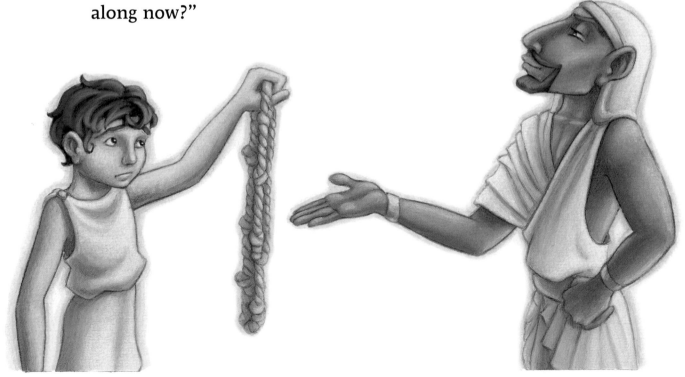

As his father and Nef talked, Pythagoras found an old piece of rope and tied knots in it. He pulled the rope into different triangles.

Finally, he made a triangle that seemed right. It had 3 lengths on one side, 4 lengths on another side, and 5 lengths on the longest side. "I've got it!" he said to himself.

Just then Pythagoras's father called him. "Carry this crate of tiles, son. Nef and I will carry the rest."

"I would carry them," Nef sighed, "but I've hurt my thumb so I can't. You'll have to make two trips."

When they got to the house Nef was building, he said, "While you get the rest of the tiles, I'll get the money I owe you." Grumbling, Pythagoras's father headed back to the ship.

Nef patted Pythagoras on the head. "Be a good boy and watch these tiles for me," he said as he disappeared into the house. "And don't touch anything!"

Pythagoras looked around the sunny courtyard. In the middle stood a statue base made of stone.

He took some tiles out of the crate just to see how they would look around the base. "I can put them back quickly," he thought.

He made a row of three red tiles along one side of the statue base. He added two more rows of red tiles, making a square.

"Some of these crates have blue tiles," Pythagoras said. Soon red and blue tiles were scattered everywhere.

Pythagoras made a square of blue tiles and a big square of red and blue tiles.

He was admiring his work when he noticed, "This statue base is a right triangle! Its sides are 3, 4, and 5 tiles long."

He counted the tiles. "Strange," he thought. "The 9 tiles in the red square plus the 16 tiles in the blue square equal 25 tiles. There are exactly 25 tiles in the big red and blue square!"

Suddenly a voice demanded, "What do you think you are doing?"

Nef rushed into the courtyard. Pythagoras's father was right behind him. "What's all this?" Nef snapped.

"I'm sorry," Pythagoras said. "I was going to put the tiles back. But I found out something interesting —"

"I don't care what you found!" interrupted Nef. "Look at this mess!"

"Pythagoras, pick up the tiles," his father said sternly. "And hurry — we have many more stops to make today."

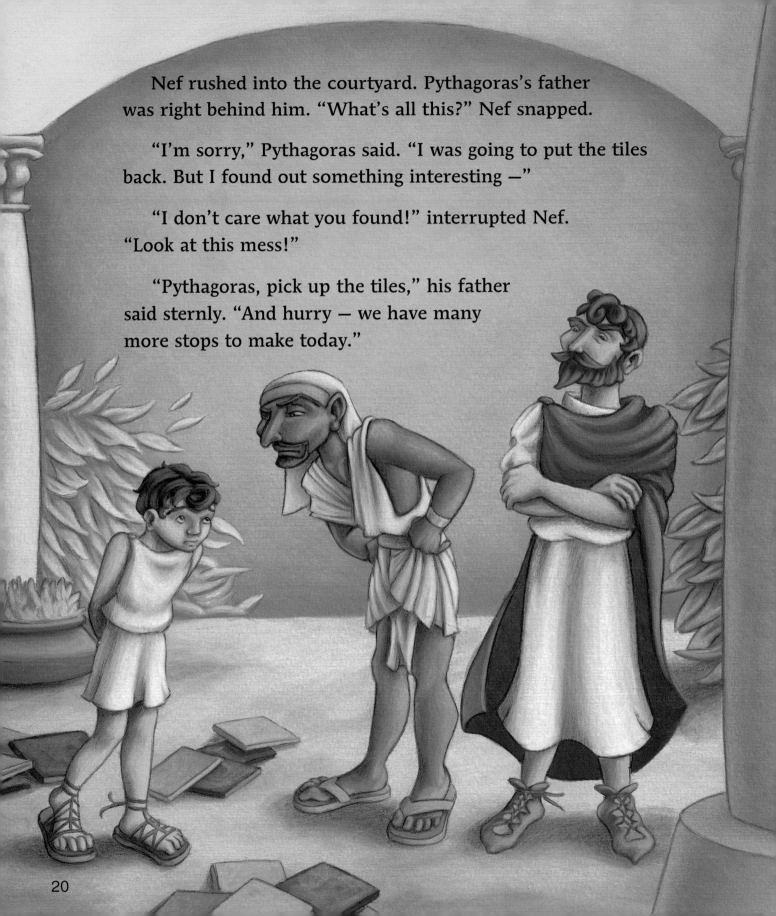

The next day, Pythagoras and his father set sail for home. To pass the time, Pythagoras drew a picture of the tile squares he had made.

"The square with 3 tiles on each side had 9 tiles, the one with 4 on each side had 16 tiles, and the one with 5 on each side had 25 tiles.

"So, in a square, the length of a side, times itself, is the number of tiles in the whole square. I'll call it 'squaring' when I multiply a number by itself. Three times three is three squared. I'll write it $3^2$."

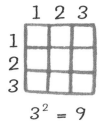

$3^2 = 9$

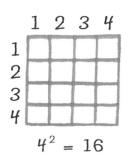

$4^2 = 16$

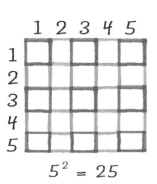

$5^2 = 25$

Pythagoras drew a new picture. "Three squared plus four squared equals five squared," he said to himself.

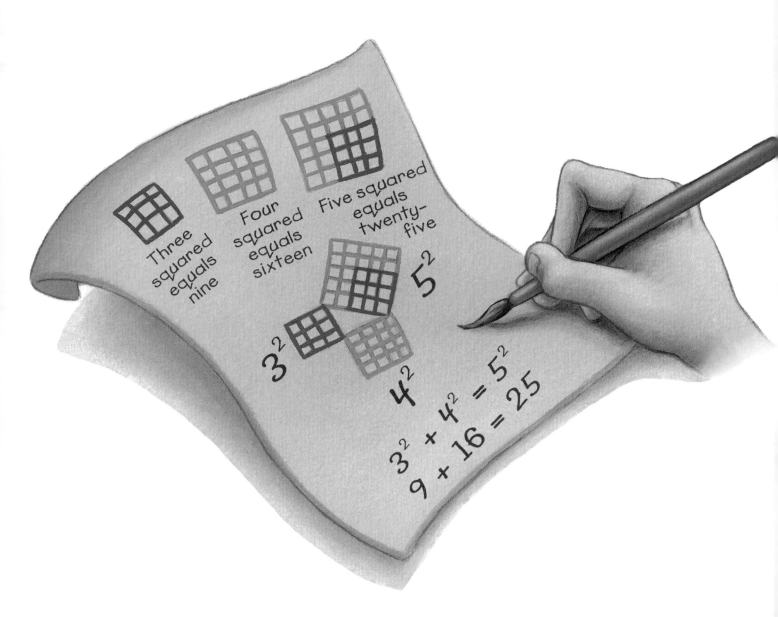

"I wonder if the squares on the sides of other right triangles add up the same way?" he thought.

Pythagoras practically flew off
the ship when he got home. He couldn't
wait to tell Saltos and Pepros about the special
knotted rope and the secret of the right triangle.

When he got to the unfinished temple, Saltos and Pepros were not there. The ladder was on the ground where Pepros had thrown it.

"That ladder would be easy to climb if the bottom were about five feet from the wall," Pythagoras thought. "Pepros said that the wall is 12 feet high."

He drew a triangle in the dirt and wrote

$$5^2 + 12^2 = ?$$
$$25 + 144 = 169$$
$$169 = 13 \times 13$$

"That's it! The ladder needs to be 13 feet long."

He fixed the ladder and headed home.

At home, Pythagoras got out a map. He looked at it closely. "I wonder . . ." he said to himself.

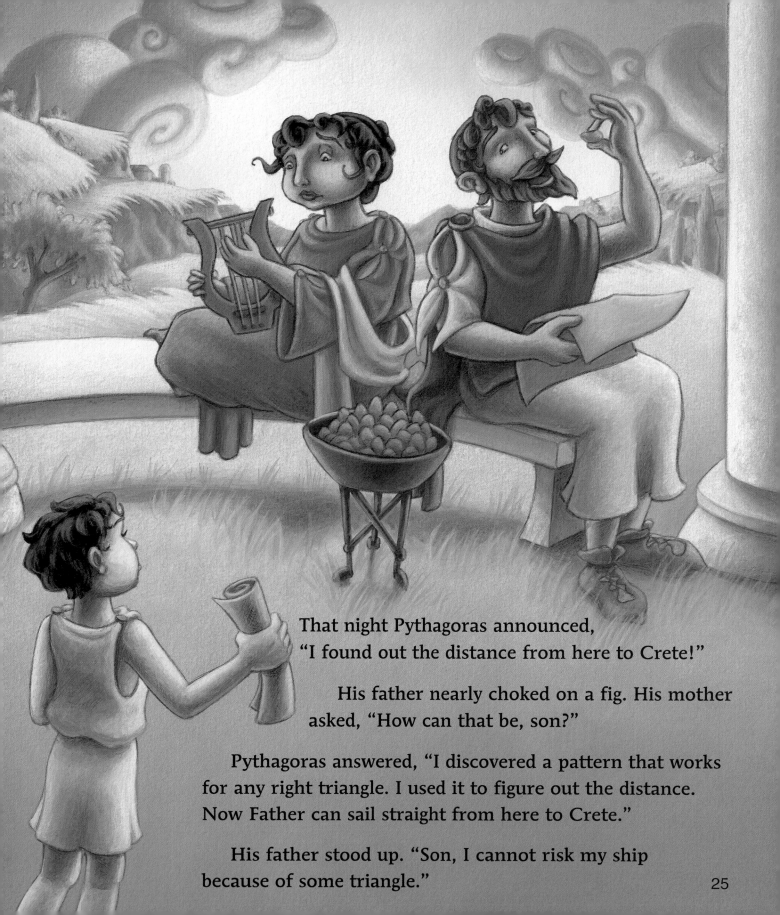

That night Pythagoras announced, "I found out the distance from here to Crete!"

His father nearly choked on a fig. His mother asked, "How can that be, son?"

Pythagoras answered, "I discovered a pattern that works for any right triangle. I used it to figure out the distance. Now Father can sail straight from here to Crete."

His father stood up. "Son, I cannot risk my ship because of some triangle."

25

"Father —" Pythagoras started to explain. At that moment, Saltos and Pepros came rushing in, puffing hard as if they had raced up the hill.

Pepros turned to Pythagoras, "You did something to our ladder!"

"Has Pythagoras been bothering you again?" his father asked, frowning.

Saltos shook his head, "No! He made our ladder the perfect length. We will be able to finish the roof now."

Pepros added, "Then all we'll have to do is fix the crooked bases of the columns."

"Maybe I can help," Pythagoras offered. "Use my rope to make right angles. If you use a right angle to make the bases straight, the columns will stand straight."

Saltos laughed. "Great! Now we can finish the temple on time. You're welcome to stop by and help us any time you like."

Pythagoras's father said, "Son, on second thought, maybe you should tell me about the distance to Crete."

Pythagoras explained, "Our island, Samos, forms a right triangle with Rhodes and Crete. If I call the sides of the triangle $a$, $b$, and $c$, I can use my right triangle pattern $a^2 + b^2 = c^2$ to figure out the distance from here to Crete."

"You can see how $a^2 + b^2$ equals 34,225.

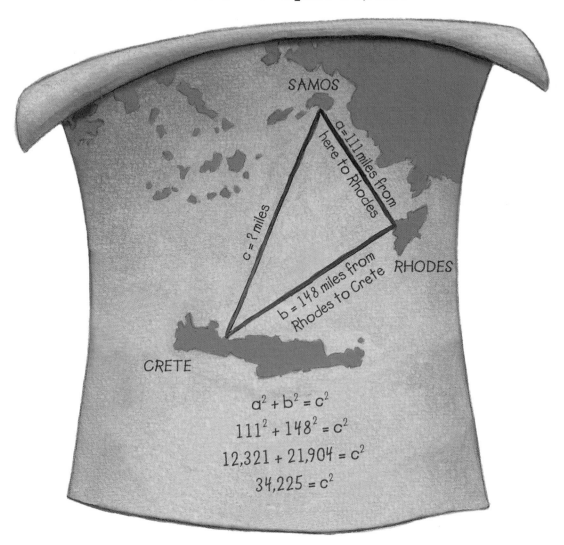

"To find *c*, the distance between here and Crete, I had to find what number multiplied by itself equals 34,225.

"I already knew $148^2$ equals 21,904. That's too small.

"I tried 200, but $200^2$ equals 40,000. That's too big.

"I tried 180, and $180^2$ equals 32,400. That's close!

"Then, I tried 185 times 185. That's exactly 34,225. So, the distance from our island to Crete is 185 miles."

Everyone was amazed. Pythagoras's father clapped him on the back. "Good thinking, son! You'll make a fine merchant someday."

Pythagoras's mother said gently, "Perhaps he can use his quick mind for other things."

His father nodded. "Son, with your clear thinking, you could be a general, a senator, a teacher, or anything you want. It's your choice."

Pythagoras smiled. He hoped to do great things in the future.